Pardon my Passion

Letters from a Serial Entrepreneur

LaKeshia Marie Gardner

ISBN: 1977579264
ISBN 13: 9781977579263
Library of Congress Control Number: 2017915042
CreateSpace Independent Publishing Platform
North Charleston, South Carolina

Contents

To the yes in a world of nos.

hy are you here?

If you don't know, I suggest you find out. Have you ever sat back and wondered what would happen if you took a leap into your destiny? If you put some effort into those things that keep you up at night and tug at your heart? We are all blessed with talents and abilities to do great things, but not many of us have the will to chase our dreams. Those of us who muster up the courage to become entrepreneurs often do so with no plan, no direction, and weak determination. It isn't until after we have bumped our heads a few times that we realize there's a process to success, and planning partnered with strength could take us to the top.

When I tapped into my passion, I had no direction. I didn't know how I would chase my dreams, but I knew I would regret not chasing them. I was a young woman with a head full of thoughts and dreams but no execution. I started two businesses and doubted my talents daily. I had a plan for new products or tools I could introduce, and instead of acting on them, I left them in the back of my thoughts. I made a list of all the reasons I would fail. I wasted years not fully believing in myself and ignoring the fire my passion lit inside me. I became lazy.

We live in a boss-or-be-bossed society. If you aren't in the position to sustain yourself, then you aren't preparing yourself for economic survival. Everyone is blessed with a unique talent, and if you decide to neglect your talent, you will never be wealthy and never truly be free. We work ourselves into our grave for someone else, accepting misery along the way. It's okay to have a job to ensure financial stability but make sure you are being wise with the finances being secured. The businesses we start for ourselves are built with the sweat equity we invest with someone else. Set a goal of securing your own so that your passion isn't neglected.

Passion is the adrenaline force pushing us toward our dreams when everything and everyone around us is convincing us to quit. It's one of the top five personality traits of success. Finding your passion is like finding the pot of gold at the end of the rainbow. Your passion can open so many doors and lead you down unimaginable paths. Passion, if followed, can bring you so much peace and so many rewards.

Everyone is trying to get somewhere or do something, and the proper process can get us all there. *Pardon My Passion* is an encouragement to the entrepreneur. From cover to cover, you can find inspiration, direction, and raw truths. The premise behind this book is to help individuals and corporate consumers unleash their unique style and successfully navigate their passions and aspirations from beginning to end. Upon completion of this book, you will be equipped with a blueprint for purposeful planning en route to your destination—a blueprint beginning with the passion that ignites you, followed by the purpose soon defined, and ending with the peace you receive as the ultimate gift for chasing your dream. This book doesn't assist in skipping the struggle or avoiding failures but is tailored to bring ease to your process.

I'm a serial entrepreneur who started this journey in 2013 with $150 of expendable funds and a dream. I had no clue how tough entrepreneurship would be. My first event client had a budget of $500 for a seventy-person event. Being eager, and naïve, I accepted the client with a huge smile on my face and decided to make it work. I spent more of my own money attempting to make the event presentable than the client was paying me. I ended the event with a satisfied client and a sad bank account. That was a learning moment for me. I knew then that I needed to research my passion and find ways to grow within my financial means. In my first year, I only had four clients. I was discouraged but not defeated. My second year gave me seven clients, and I was grateful for each one. In 2015 I began graphic designing and finding ways to give my clients a one-stop shopping experience.

My second business was born in 2016 when I was being paid to design and make T-shirts more than I was being booked for events. I've always been a fan of multiple streams of income, so I welcomed the new responsibilities. There were many times I wanted to give up. I'd celebrate a win only to prepare for the next loss. Had I given up on my passion and talents, I wouldn't be in the place I am today. In 2017 I've been booked at least two weekends every month. I've designed numerous T-shirts, gifts, and printed materials. Although my first client had a budget of $500, I've been fortunate to work with clients who have budgets in the upper tens of thousands of dollars. Keeping with my serial entrepreneur hustle, in 2017 I expanded my events business to offer linen rentals and custom design packages. Entrepreneurs don't quit. We revise, revamp, and start completely over if we have to. I have two businesses that I'm very proud of and look forward to growing to new heights; however, my next goal is to inspire other people like me. Sometimes we need encouragement to step into entrepreneurship, and I hope my book does that for you.

After reading and utilizing this book, I hope you will walk away inspired and excited about your entrepreneurial journey. This book handles the aspects often forgotten and grants you the peace of mind necessary to enjoy your journey. I hope that you will find enjoyment in the process. Implement the Triple S System into your grind. It takes most millionaires eleven years or more to make their first million...what are you waiting for?

Entrepreneurship is living a few years of your life like most people will not so you can spend the rest of your life like most people cannot.

—*Student (unidentified) of Warren G. Tracy*

Sell

Hello, Dream Chaser

Your time is money, so sell it; do not give it away for free or cheap.

Wake Up

I was rounding out the third week of my second-to-last class in my doctoral program, and boy, was I beat! I thanked the Lord with each keystroke that I had a Memorial Day/birthday vacation planned with my best friend. My trip finally arrived, but I wasn't out of the scholarly woods yet. You see, on the doctoral level, they don't care about vacations or crises. You better have that assignment turned in by the due date, or you'll be paying to take that class again. Since I understood that, my MacBook accompanied me on my trip.

The first night there, after spending some time on the beach, I decided to get some homework done before we enjoyed the nightlife. I submitted my discussions and had a night to remember. The next morning, I was lying in bed and decided to check my school e-mail from my phone (I was serious about completing this degree). My heart sank into my stomach when I saw an e-mail from my professor stating I hadn't submitted a two-hundred-point assignment the week before. Imagine spending days on a ten-page paper and having your professor tell you she doesn't have it. I instantly logged on to my portal and saw it hanging in limbo in the submission software. My professor logged in and saw the same and allowed me to e-mail her the assignment.

Now, normally that would be the ending to a feel-good story, but this is where the drama began. I attempted to power on my MacBook that had worked just fine the night before, only to see that it was overheating and not fully loading. I panicked. I hadn't been backing up my work for months on anything other than that MacBook. Yes, I know better than that, but *life*. I justified my lack of not backing up my work by stating I was "too busy." Too busy transitioned to too pissed just like that. If it were to die, I thought I would too. *Everything* about my extensive doctoral study and my personal endeavors (like this book) were on that MacBook. I surrendered to defeat and cried while I drank Stella Rosa with the Kehlani Pandora station blasting in the background until I was numb.

It's those periods of unnecessary and wasteful numbness that teach you the most. I had so much time to think and no tools to react. As I sat there staring at the beach with tears in my eyes and wine on my breath, my mind wandered to some of the innermost places. I was so close to the edge that I allowed something as simple as a technical issue to completely unhinge me. For what? I woke up every day and reported to a job that I did well, although it stressed me out. I bore the burdens that came with the job, so the "powers that be" didn't have to. I went to school to better myself while allowing the process to break me down. Yet when it came to my entrepreneurial endeavors, I tiptoed. I procrastinated, I made excuses, and I walked away without putting up the slightest bit of fight. I had to remind myself that if I were trying to become one of those "powers that be" people, I needed to act like it.

How is it that we allow ourselves to go through the fire for everyone and everything else besides ourselves and our dreams? That miserable moment in the midst of a great trip was my moment of clarity. It was time for me to start really exercising the things I believed in and preached to others. The time to trust my passion process was now.

Set the problems aside, and remind yourself that it's okay to be great. The fact is bad things are going to happen. You just need to make sure you have conditioned your IDGAF demeanor so that it can kick in when necessary. Discomfort should become a habit. Discomfort causes you to get up, get out, and get to work. Your calling can be simple, or it can be grand. The beauty of it all is that we each have one. Stop convincing yourself that you don't deserve to explore your self-made options. Stop focusing on what you believe you "should be doing" and secure that bag.

I returned home and found out the MacBook was dead. To make things worse, nothing could be pulled off the hard drive. But God! My assignment was accessible through the portal, and I had a backup copy of my doctoral study and my book. The impossible is possible when you move like a boss. Sometimes it just takes a little patience and for you to calm the heck down. Your life and situations aren't going to change themselves. You have to choose every single day to be better, to do better, and to live better. The time that I lost in tears and sorrow was the last I had to give. I decided that I would step into day one instead of waiting for one day. Now it's your turn.

What is your why?

Take a moment to explore your why. It's important moving forward that you have your "why" established and you are able to reflect on the words in my letters. Below list your why, your drive, your passion and your goals.

_____

_____

_____

_____

_____

_____

_____

_____

_____

_____

_____

_____

_____

_____

_____

_____

_____

_____

_____

_____

_____

_____

_____

_____

_____

_____

_____

_____

_____

_____

_____

_____

_____

_____

_____

_____

_____

_____

_____

_____

_____

_____

_____

_____

Stop making excuses and start making things happen.

—J.J. Watts, Professional Athlete

Cultivating Soil

$\mathcal{I}$ remember spending summers at my great-grandmother's house and admiring all the potted plants she had set up in her sunroom. You know that one section of the house right off the kitchen with the big window and fancy china? The area of the house the kids aren't allowed to go unless given specific instructions to do so? Although I could not venture into that space, I could not help but admire it every time I walked by. My great-grandmother had what they called "growing hands." If you gave her anything green or seed and some soil, she could make it grow. The irony in my great-grandmother's "growing hands" is that it was not her hands that caused her plants to thrive. It was the time, attention, and concern she placed on those plants that yielded the beauty.

When we would get scratched and scraped up from being kids, she'd send us to the plants. I'll never forget breaking off a piece of aloe to take some of the pain from my adventures away. There was healing in some of her plants, and she knew just which one to send you to for you to get exactly what you needed. Because of the time and care, she had placed in those plants, she was sure that they could get the job done.

To be successful as an entrepreneur, you need to develop a set of growing hands. When faced with failures and periods of little to no growth, we are quick to complain and blame everything and everyone around us. Truth be told, we should be looking at what we could've done differently to ensure we were ready to grow. Did we check the condition of our soil before planting our seeds? Were we prepared to give time, attention, and concern to our dreams?

Nothing but weeds can grow from bad soil. It's a common misconception that the only thing needed to assist the soil in the growth process is water. Although water is essential, without air the roots aren't able to receive the essentials to play their part in the growth and sustainability process. The best way to get air to your roots is to cultivate your soil. During the cultivation process, the soil is lightly broken in all the right places, removing the crusty soil and any other elements preventing growth. By placing your seed in cultivated soil, you are preparing it for rapid growth and ensuring that whatever blooms will do so at its full potential.

When chasing after your dreams, visualize yourself as the soil and your dreams as the seeds preparing to grow. Before planting any of your dreams, make sure you are prepared to do the work necessary for growth. Cultivate yourself and remove any hindrance or doubt that could keep air from reaching the roots of your dreams. Stop planting great things in dirty soil. Dirty soil returns short-lived beauty riddled with weeds. It causes doubt and delays success. The destination you are headed toward has no room for doubt. Put the proper amount of time into yourself so that when your journey scratches and scrapes you up, you can break off a piece of motivation, energy, or drive to take the pain away and push you forward. Determine how badly you want to get there, cultivate your soil, and witness the growth.

What's your soil looking like?
Take a moment to assess your current climate. What are your surrounds and how can you give more time to your growth and passion process. Start below by listing simple steps.

_____

_____

_____

_____

_____

_____

_____

_____

_____

_____

_____

_____

_____

_____

_____

_____

The secret to getting ahead is getting started.

—Mark Twain, Writer

Destination Preparation

*I*t all starts with an idea—a gut-churning set of thoughts that sends your mind in circles and initially will not let you rest. This happens within each of us. The magic after that is dependent upon what you do with these thoughts. An idea is just a thought until you place the pen to the paper.

Write your vision or idea down—not just the good parts but every single detail. Scribble it if you must, but make sure you write it down. It's far too easy to get lost in distraction and lose your train of thought. Never let a good idea pass you by because you were not prepared or were too preoccupied to document it. Once I realized the entrepreneurial spirit in me, I began sleeping with a notebook by my bed and keeping a tablet in my purse. I wanted to make sure that whenever that great idea or inspiration hit me, I could write it down.

A well-thought-out and well-documented idea is the foundation to any great plan. This is true for life and business planning. You may have an important life goal or accomplishment that has been on your mind for quite some time. Write it down. Look at it daily until you are ready to construct the steps and details necessary to get you to the point of completion or achievement. If there's a business, you would like to start or a milestone you would like to reach, write it down. Take the time to research the market, and design a plan that can get you there.

Once you have written down your ideas and plans, it's important that you not let the ink go to waste. Ink on paper means nothing if there's no action. There are hundreds of thousands of free tools and tons of information available to assist you with anything you desire to attempt. Don't be afraid to ask someone for direction; however, you should be cautious. Your dreams, plans, visions, and goals aren't meant for everyone. Don't invite the public to a private table until the table has been properly set.

Pen to paper is a phrase that symbolizes the permanence of ink. Just like the ink on a sheet of paper, your deep-seated dreams and desires are permanent. You can strike them out, scribble over them, rip them up, water them down, or rub them out, but with the right amount of focus, they become clear—the same as the day they sat in your spirit, and you wrote them down. They will appear to you once again as clear as ever. Most people don't find the value in a dream. They don't realize the importance. A person who doesn't dream has no vision or hope. A person who doesn't acknowledge his or her dreams is forsaking his or her vision and hope. By not positioning yourself to invest in your dreams or at least seek them out, you are unintentionally positioning yourself to sow someone else's visions and dreams daily. There may be someone out there doing something similar to what you believe you could do, but I guarantee you they can't do it the way you can. There's room for us all at the table of success; you just have to be prepared to take your seat.

Write your vision.

What is it you desire to do? What great business or services can you provide?

_____

_____

_____

_____

_____

_____

_____

_____

_____

_____

_____

_____

_____

_____

_____

_____

_____

_____

_____

I'm convinced that about half of what separates the successful entrepre-neurs from the non-successful ones is pure perseverance.

—Steve Jobs, Co-Founder of Apple

Beautiful Discomfort

When chasing a dream and growing toward your potential, the initial stages are spent in what can be viewed as a "pot." A "pot" is a one-size-fits-all temporary container that ensures you aren't disturbed or displaced in your fragile state. You become comfortable in this space. It's all you have grown to know. There has been success in your "pot," and you have grown a great deal. But now comes the time to experience beautiful discomfort. It's time to be uprooted from the comforts of your "pot" and placed in a larger environment, where things are unknown, and potential is amplified. During this transfer process, you are shaken, and parts of you are broken off because they can't go where you are going. You have cultivated your soil and developed strong roots, but along the way, those roots have gotten tangled. Too much time spent in the "pot" will hinder your growth and begin to interfere with your foundation.

Break off the tangled portions of your roots, and get ready for increase. Your dreams are too important and too big for you to find solace with a "pot" mentality. The beauty of discomfort is it gives you no other choice but to fight your way back to the comfort zone. Adapt to the changes, and watch your dreams grow to levels without limits. Dreams are not "one size fits all." Don't give a temporary setting permanent benefits.

You may not like the process of growth during your journey, and it most likely will not be comfortable. If success is what you desire, the process is necessary. There will always be change in business. Make the decision to not handicap your dreams. Uproot as things change and move to a new pot. Increase is a good thing, and those that grow through it receive their rewards.

What's your comfort zone?
What changes in your current routine or current business endeavors frighten you? What do you plan to do to grow through those periods of discomfort?

_____

_____

_____

_____

_____

_____

_____

_____

_____

_____

_____

_____

_____

_____

_____

_____

_____

_____

Waiting for perfect is never as smart as making progress.

—Seth Godin, Author

Fantasy versus Reality

Chiavari chairs, sequin backdrops, and elaborate florals—those are the things I saw when I closed my eyes and envisioned my events. I would see these elaborate setups on Instagram, designed by event specialists I admired, and want that to be me. Reaching that level of detail is possible; however, it takes time, connections, money, and clients. In the beginning, I had none of the above. It's easy to look at an established company or small business and say, "I want to be just like them." The mind is taking a mental picture of what could be; however, it's our responsibility to assess what we are seeing and separate the reality from the fantasy. While you are taking in the elegance and achievement being displayed, it's important to acknowledge the time those people invested and the obstacles they overcame to get to where they are. It's very possible to reach the heights of some of the businesses and companies you admire; however, the reality is, you must be ready to put in the work.

Fantasy has an appealing way of convincing us to make decisions prematurely. Approaching a dream or endeavor without proper planning or assessment can cause unnecessary heartache. Entrepreneurs are some of the most passionate and hardworking people on the face of the earth, in my opinion, and it isn't uncommon for an entrepreneur to want to put the cart before the horse. This is where a fantasy-versus-reality situation comes into play. Fantasy will tell you to run full force toward your dreams, while reality will encourage you to run but take breaks for direction along the way.

Reality has a redeeming quality to it. Reality allows us to see the bigger picture and what needs to be done to get us there. As a means of encouragement and drive, it's essential to allow fantasy to remain on the team while remembering reality is the coach. Some of the biggest letdowns came from me focusing too hard on the fantasy of my dreams as opposed to the reality of them. Once I took a step back and assessed things from a realistic perspective, my road to completion became clearer. I decided not to dwell on the loss of time fantasy granted me, but to instead celebrate the lessons learned. A key piece of advice that I always share is, "A good entrepreneur indulges in fantasy, but a great entrepreneur sees the value in reality."

You have to give your dreams time to unfold. Set the goal you want to reach and watch it develop as you take the necessary steps. We live in a social era where media meant to keep us connected, often leads us to comparison and self-doubt. The quickest way to ensure your business or idea won't take off is to spend time focusing on other entrepreneurs and comparing yourself. The reality in their business isn't the reality of yours. You could be that dope, that grand, that popular, and that great, you're just going to have to put in the work for it. Find the value in where you start, what you have, and who you are. Fantasy will always be there. Reality is waiting for you to make your next move.

What's your Reality?

What are you currently working on to push your gift forward? If you haven't started the work, list why.

_____

_____

_____

_____

_____

_____

_____

_____

_____

_____

_____

_____

_____

_____

_____

_____

_____

_____

_____

_____

If you're going through hell, keep going.

—*Winston Churchill, British Prime Minister*

Dream Killers

Now, I know you are expecting this section to begin with a catchy line signifying the lack of support from those closest to you; however, that isn't necessary. The bottom line is, you are good enough. You are strong enough. You are smart enough. You are blessed enough. God equipped you with everything you needed to be successful on this earth the day he laid your passion on you.

A dream killer is any person, situation, or circumstance that deters you from your dream. Dream killers have one goal, and that's to make sure you fail. Anyone chasing a dream or building a business has encountered or will encounter a few dream killers along the way. It isn't your place to understand a dream killer. By investing time in matters that are working against you, you are doing the work for them. The more time you invest in the negative, the less time you have for your dreams and endeavors. A dream killer can't help being whom or what they are, but you have 100 percent control over how you respond. One of the most fundamental lessons I learned when I began my entrepreneurial journey was not to waste time focusing on the elements working against me. I would find myself getting so angry because those I entrusted to be there for me were some of the key dream killers during my journey. I would analyze their actions and complain about how they were treating me, and all that did was deter me from my dreams and cause me to question my own success. Will it upset you, yes, but what it won't do is stop you, unless you let it.

There I was, considering walking away from my passion and settling for "the norm" when I realized the dream killers were about to win. The dream killers were so good at their job that they convinced me to kill my dreams on my own. If a dream killer can invest the time to complete the task of bringing me down, I could invest double the amount of time in ensuring I was a success. That type of thinking allows you to view the various dream killers in your life as motivators and opportunities. Every day, work twice as hard to begin eliminating the dream killers in your life. If your dream killer is a person or a group of people, work so hard that they begin to admire you. Give them no choice but to have positive affirmations when it comes to your endeavors. If your dream killer is a situation, remove yourself. Set aside the necessary time, no more or less, to assess the situation, and decide on the best way to remove yourself from it. Circumstances change daily, and there's no reason for anyone to allow a circumstance to keep them from their dreams.

Sit yourself down, and ask if the vision you have comes from God. If your answer is yes, then you must realize that no weapon formed against you shall prosper. The uncanny thing about dream killers is that they never actually kill your dream. Dream killers are so good at what they were designed to do that they convince you to kill the dream yourself. Distractions, upsets, delays, rejections, and objections are tools used by dream killers to push you into a space of unachievable goals. Never allow something that keeps you up at night to be put to bed by anything other than completion.

Can you focus on me?
Me being your goals, your passion, your gift. List the dream killers you
have and the ways you can remove your focus from them.

_____

_____

_____

_____

_____

_____

_____

_____

_____

_____

_____

_____

_____

_____

_____

_____

_____

_____

_____

_____

I hated every minute of training, but I said, "Don't quit. Suffer now and live the rest of your life as a champion."

—*Muhammad Ali, Boxing Champion*

Strategy, Please

If there had to be a common weakness among most entrepreneurs, it would have to be the absence of strategic planning. It's common to have an idea and instinctively want to act on it for fear of delaying the process. In some cases, this may work; however, if your goal is success and longevity, a strategic plan is essential. Your efforts to plan effectively and strategically don't have to be elaborate or costly. There are many free ways to develop a strategic plan for success and get your business or idea off the ground.

My advice to starter entrepreneurs is to assess their market partners. I use the term "market partners" instead of "competition" because "competition" holds a different meaning to me than it may to others. If I'm assessing a business I admire and would like to model my business after, it isn't my competition. It's merely a business in my market that I view as a partner I can learn from. To compete with someone, you have to be in the arena. As a start-up event-planning business, your competition isn't David Tutera. To bring it down a notch, your competition isn't even the leading planner in your city. You shouldn't assess them as someone you would like to compete with, but as someone, you can learn from. Thus, you have "market partners" in place of competitors. I'm a firm believer in the phrase, "There's enough out here for everyone."

Whatever you decide to do, you do it your very best and give it your all. When you plan your business to function in that capacity, the only competition you should have is yourself.

Assessing the business market is a free advancement and planning tool you should arm yourself with. The information available is plentiful. You simply must be willing to put in the hard work and long hours to define how the information can benefit the business or idea you are trying to bring to life. When assessing the market and gathering information, I would suggest you keep your search narrow in the beginning. If your search is broad, you may be gathering information that might not pertain to the route you desire to travel, and it can cause confusion.

Confusion in the beginning stages of business development is the primary cause of delays and doubts. Starting a business is hard enough; don't complicate it by overloading yourself with information. My suggestion is to find a business model that can be converted to support the business you are developing and proceed from there. Ask questions. There are many entrepreneurs and business owners who don't mind sharing pieces of information with someone looking to develop his or her ideas. Not everyone will be willing to share information for free, so don't be offended by those who choose to redirect your efforts. Learn to respect the fact that they are business owners, and it's simply business, not personal. Don't get discouraged by those who choose not to share their information, because there are many out there who are happy to pour wisdom into others. If the majority of your free-business-advice efforts fail, remember, Google is your friend.

Finding a business mentor is essential to strategic plan development. When starting a business, many of us are so quick to share our dreams with friends and family, thinking they will share our excitement and have positive advice. It can be disheartening to learn that that's often not the case. That doesn't mean your family and friends don't want you to succeed; it simply points to the notion that those who don't have the same entrepreneurial desires as you may not process things the way you do. This is where a business mentor comes into play. Someone who is in business or building a business will understand your desires, frustrations, visions, and failures. It's important to have someone in your corner whom you trust and can run ideas by. Because they too are branching out into the world of entrepreneurship, or may already be there, they are more inclined to give you that backing and push you need.

I'll never forget how I met my business mentor. My mentor happened to be in the same industry I was trying to break into, yet she chose to push me further than I could've ever pushed myself. In my situation, I knew I needed some guidance, but I was very apprehensive about trusting others with my vision. After suffering failures in trying to gain momentum, I was losing faith in myself and my business. I figured adding someone successful to the equation would only add fuel to the fire. Fortunately for me, God had other plans, and he sent my mentor to me.

Natasha Kendle of the Kendle Group, now based out of Northwest Arkansas, saw me at a Black Women Helping Black Women event in Little Rock, Arkansas and decided she wanted to be connected to me and make sure I didn't give up. In the meeting, they allowed us to share our stories and ask questions if we had areas where we were suffering. I expressed my sentiments and took my seat ready to note the feedback I received. I received many encouraging words and new ways to approach my business endeavors. I left that meeting with a new outlook and positive thoughts about moving forward. However, it was not the meeting that changed my business perspective; it was the call that followed.

I left the meeting early because I had to rush off to other commitments. At that time, I was pursing my MBA and needed to get to class. While in class, I received a message from one of my friends who attended the meeting with me, stating there was a lady by the name of Natasha who wanted to speak with me, and she had asked for my number. I was puzzled as to why she wanted to speak to me but honored as well. Natasha called me that night and changed my business for the better. She saw something in me that I had not yet seen in myself. Natasha took the time not only to encourage and motivate me but also to extend herself to me. When I want to give up, when I suffer a failure, when I have a question, I can go to Natasha. She has been one of the primary driving forces behind my relentless chase of my entrepreneurial dreams. When I told her I was writing a book, she was excited! Anyone else may have questioned my knowledge or what made me believe I was capable of writing a self-help book when I've yet to make it to the peak of my career. Not Natasha. Natasha saw the passion behind my efforts and understood how my message could help someone. Natasha came into my life as a complete stranger and is now a part of my family—loved by everyone in my family, but me the most. I'll forever treasure her, and no matter how large I become, she will forever be my mentor and an essential part of my strategic plan. If you're serious about this journey, you'll need a Natasha.

The final resources that I suggest are paid training and education. You must invest in your dreams for them to flourish. Training and education in the market you are interested in are beneficial in more ways than you can imagine. Attend the training, and take from them the gems necessary to grow your business. Develop your own methods using your training as inspiration, and you will see great results.

Training doesn't have to be extremely costly. Often we believe that we need to attend the major events and training being hosted by the highly sought-after entrepreneurs and industry leaders, but when you are new to the business, that isn't going to be a good investment. Many of the things taught in those types of courses are for entrepreneurs who have been at it a while and may need additional guidance to get them to the next level. My recommendation is to find training that offers detailed business-development information and a welcoming environment that leaves the door open for networking and guidance along the way. These personable and structured environments allow you to be transparent and open up. In doing that, you can receive a personalized response and experience. I find it easier to relate to an everyday person like myself, who saw a dream and chased it. That person's story relates to mine, and his or her approach tends to yield a lasting result.

As you may notice, I've given you advice on approaches to strategic planning instead of a detailed step-by-step guide. I've learned over the years that there's no copy-and-paste approach to developing a detailed strategic plan for your business. Your business is *your business*, and I can't tailor the process for you. There are many resources out there that do that, and I urge you to consult them during the outlining process. The tools and direction I've provided are meant to be your foundation while you construct your strategic plan. Everything isn't always black and white, and I hope that my recommendations add some color to your bigger picture.

What's the plan?
So, I gave you steps and suggestions, how do they apply to you?

_____

_____

_____

_____

_____

_____

_____

_____

_____

_____

_____

_____

_____

_____

_____

_____

_____

_____

_____

_____
_____
_____
_____
_____
_____
_____
_____
_____
_____
_____
_____
_____
_____
_____
_____
_____
_____
_____
_____
_____

100 percent of the shots you don't take, don't go in.

—Wayne Gretzky, Hockey Legend

Busy versus Effective

Have you ever encountered someone who was always busy, always doing something, always swamped but never harvested fruits from all that labor? Don't be that person! If you're already that person, it's not too late to switch things up. I can honestly admit that use to be me. I'd have so many things I was trying to attack at once that none of them ended up getting the attention they needed or deserved. I had to become disciplined and turn my sticky notes into lists or taskers that I could follow up on. The simple difference between busy and effectiveness is the outcome. Did you come to a stage of completion, or was your labor in vain?

As an entrepreneur, it's important for your busy work to be effective. There are no set hours for entrepreneurs, and it's important that we make every minute of every day count for something. What good is it to be busy and have nothing to show for it? If your efforts aren't effective, the only profit you make from being busy is a tired soul. When you make the decision to dedicate your time, energy, and attention to a task, make sure the end result will add to your business journey and not take away from it. An effective entrepreneur is a consistent entrepreneur. You may not be where you hope to be, but if you are seeing results, you are destined to continue on your path. The misconception comes from us being taught to remain busy at all times. Every day, we hear phrases about idle minds and wasted time, and once the brain processes those phrases, it urges us not to fall into that category. Remaining busy while building a business or chasing a dream is important, but it's equally important to be effective in your efforts. Work smarter, not harder. Remember that you want to enjoy your process and not place more on yourself than you can bear.

In the beginning stages of my entrepreneurial journey, I made the mistake of believing I had to remain busy at all times, without realizing I was getting nowhere. I was extremely tired and frustrated because of this. I had to realize that every business fad and task was not meant for me and my businesses. I had to decipher the effective methods from the ineffective methods and funnel my energy in the right direction. Now, I pay more attention to the moves that will make an impact and push my businesses that much closer to where I aspire them to be. I transitioned from being a constantly busy entrepreneur to an effective entrepreneur who was not only building businesses but also building positive client relationships along the way. In the battle of busy versus effective, it's important that you lean toward the effective momentum in the early stages to avoid many hours of waste and regret. Everything doesn't have to be a learning experience.

Are you effective?

If you aren't tired for a purpose, then the answer is no. List habits you need to change to make sure you're effectively attacking your tasks and goals.

_____

_____

_____

_____

_____

_____

_____

_____

_____

_____

_____

_____

_____

_____

_____

_____

_____

_____

Work hard, be kind, and amazing things will happen.

—Conan O'Brien, Talk Show Host

"Vu Jà Dé"

Society loves a routine—a familiar schedule or turn of events that keeps us on track. In business, especially entrepreneurship, there's power in a "vu jà dé" moment. "Vu jà dé" is the opposite of *déjà vu*; it presents a familiar situation as new. A "vu jà dé" moment exposes the opportunities and possibilities hidden within a familiar situation. It gives you a fresh perspective and makes you aware of elements no one else has noticed. As an entrepreneur, a fresh spin on a familiar topic or product is equivalent to a golden ticket. The stigma of doing something that has already been done prevents the advancement of entrepreneurial endeavors. It's important that you transform an idea or business and make it unique to you. There may be hundreds of beauty suppliers in your area or market, but none of them can supply your customers as you can. I say your customers because what is for you is for you, and once you step out there, there will be a customer base ready to support you.

Each of us has been given gifts and talents. Although your products may be like someone else's, your talent to present and develop those products is totally unique. Examine your routine, examine your situation, and allow yourself a "vu jà dé" moment. At that moment, you will be provided with the opportunity to transform and enhance your business or idea.

What's new?
Your presentation is different, list why.

Spend

By Design

Now that you make more; you better learn how to spend less. Spend smart and see how far your dreams go.

Surviving the Jump

ut did you die? This is a common phrase my friends, and I use when we overly dramatize a situation that we are capable of bouncing back from. Failure and entrepreneurship go hand in hand. There's no straight path to success in entrepreneurship, so you must be prepared for and be able to accept failure. Before the steps, there's the jump—the scary and questionable jump into an arena where you have no comforts. The jump presents many factors for worry and discouragement, but you will survive. For you to survive the jump, you must place trust in yourself and trust in the process. Entrepreneurs tend to make the mistake of trying to avoid the struggle or trying to fast-track the process. There's no struggle-free path to success. You will work hard, you will make mistakes, and you will fail, but most importantly, you will survive.

Don't allow the turbulence of the jump to distract you from the journey ahead. Think of yourself as a skydiver jumping into a sky of opportunities. It's corny, I know, but stay with me. We have all seen how it plays out on television and in the movies. Before the jump, there's hesitation, fear, and second-guessing. The skydiver dared to approach the opportunity. The courage led him or her to gear up and board the plane. So why now would he or she allow fear to prevent him or her from reaching a goal and checking an item off his or her bucket list? It's human nature to have fear and to second-guess decisions. Those who choose to stick to the plan and not be often swayed experience achievement.

After encouragement and self-reflection, the skydiver jumps! Initially, the path is turbulent. Wind smacks him or her in the face, and he or she is in unfamiliar territory. As the skydiver picks up speed, things below begin to appear clear and familiar. He or she feels an early sense of pride, joy, and accomplishment. He or she draws closer and closer to the target and begins to pull back and prepare for a successful landing. Once the skydiver lands, it's time for him or her to celebrate overcoming fear and reaching the target.

The same wisdom can be applied to the entrepreneurial process. We gear ourselves up and make it to the plane; however, while onboard, we allow the success of others and the doubts within to cause us to second-guess our decision. If only we would jump! Those who silence the noise and take that jump reap the benefits of survival. Initially, there will be things that smack you in the face, and the environment will be unfamiliar, but as you continue, it will get better. You will begin to pick up speed and accomplish growth within your business. The environment will become familiar, and you will grow happier in your decision. You will then be closer to your target, allowing you to pull back and focus on the final details. You will land and look around at the business you have built or the idea you have birthed, and you will celebrate. You will celebrate your victory over fear and the great things to come. There will have been many unfamiliar experiences along the way, but in the end, you will survive.

Just jump.
What is holding you back from being great? List your fears and ways to overcome them.

_____

_____

_____

_____

_____

_____

_____

_____

_____

_____

_____

_____

_____

_____

_____

_____

_____

_____

_____

Good business leaders create a vision, articulate the vision, passionately own the vision, and relentlessly drive it to completion.

—Jack Welch, Former CEO of GE

Clarity

hasing your dreams and embracing your passion often gives you a sense of purpose. During your process, there's a moment of clarity when your dreams outline the person you are and were meant to become. We were each created with unique talents that lead us to our purpose in life. Purpose can take you far if you let it. It's an amazing feeling to know you are doing what God has placed breath in your body to do. Operating within your purpose is the expectation of the entrepreneur. Don't let things such as money, desires, or jealously persuade you to step into entrepreneurship. If your heart isn't in your efforts, your efforts will be in vain.

Clarity isn't the sole benefit of walking in your purpose. Along with clarity, you will find happiness, power, and a sense of fulfillment. The happiness that comes with following your dreams is one that can't be explained. You will not always succeed, and the transition will not be smooth, but you will find happiness in the process because you are charting your own course. Power yields a positive mind-set. A strong sense of purpose and the push needed to continue your journey come from power. Clarity allows you to dig deep and unleash your inner power.

It's important to understand your purpose and to find the value in it. Think of what the world would be like if we didn't walk in our purpose. If no one chased his or her dreams and took those steps toward entrepreneurial independence, where would we be? A life of purpose is a life well lived. Purpose gives you a feeling of importance and belonging. My moment of clarity was a pivotal turning point in my entrepreneurial endeavors. It changed the way I looked at my life and the steps I was taking toward following my dreams. I had enough passion to fill a football stadium three times over, but my purpose was unclear. I chased my dreams with my passions on the forefront, but that could only take me so far. Realizing my purpose turned the tables in my journey. Move forward until every fiber in your being gives way, and after that, continue to move. After you have given all you can, and you still have the urge to go on, that's when you have found your purpose. Purpose gives you strength that can't be explained. In that moment of clarity, you have been given a gift.

What is your gift?

What is special about you? What pushes you forward when you want to give up?

_____

_____

_____

_____

_____

_____

_____

_____

_____

_____

_____

_____

_____

_____

_____

_____

_____

_____

Never work for just money or power. That won't save your soul or help you sleep at night.

—Marian Wright Edelman, Activist

Profit Mind-Set

While others might have love on the brain, entrepreneurs tend to have money on the brain. Not just what is coming in, but what is going out as well. In the beginning stages, it's typical to want to hold on to your money when the numbers start to add up. The saying goes, "It costs to be the boss," and it holds its weight. When building a business or launching an idea, it's possible not to see any true profit until your third year. Now, I'm not saying it's impossible to see profits sooner than year three—I'm merely setting a basic expectation. In the beginning years of your business or idea development, at minimum, 33% of your profits should flow back into the business so that you may continue to expand. Another 33% should be placed into savings for obstacles that may come or larger investments you may want to make. If you work hard and invest wisely, you will see a return on your investments. Don't allow yourself to get so hung up on how much chasing your dream is costing you. Money causes problems in most aspects of life; don't allow it to cause problems in your business.

When selecting vendors or services for your business, it's okay to shop around. Have meetings, do your research, and ask around to find the right fit financially. When considering finances, remember to acknowledge quality. A cheap product that looks cheap serves no purpose. Make yourself a checklist of things you absolutely must invest in to get your business or idea off the ground. Outside of that list, all other matters are secondary. Pace yourself. There's no need to cause yourself financial hardship while chasing your dream. A broke business with a broke owner doesn't have much to offer anyone. Some choose to save enough revenue to pay all their business expenses upfront, and others choose to pay as they go. Whichever method you select, make sure you are wise in your spending and realistic in your expectations.

Waiting until you are in the perfect financial space to launch your business or idea could cause you to miss your opportunity. There's no guarantee that the opportunities of today will be there tomorrow so I would advise any budding entrepreneur to strike while the iron is hot. Follow your list, and cut back on frivolous spending in your personal life to invest in your dreams. With success comes sacrifice, and entrepreneurs know sacrifice all too well. A great way to structure your spending is to utilize a budget. A budget can alleviate the stressors attributed to business start-ups. You can stay on track and feel comfortable in your investment.

Great things come to those who budget! Budgets and business have a way of making the world go round. Okay, maybe I'm giving too much credit to the effectiveness of a budget, but I'm definitely an advocate of a good budget. A budget allows you to track your spending and plan with what you actually have. A budget is a working document with moveable parts. This means it can go up or down, left or right to accommodate the business needs.

The magic comes into play when you can find extra money or savings within the budget. Case in point: You decide that you want to allot $1,000 for marketing expenses. In your "business" mind, you have already written off that $1,000. While searching for an amazing graphic designer to bring your marketing materials to life, you find a package that suits all your needs for $750. Poof! Magic! You now have $250 extra within your budget that can be used for the advancement of your business or saved for a need you may or may not have in the future. Don't outspend your budget. If there's something you desire that falls outside the preset budget, it's time to sit down and revisit the budget to make adjustments. There's no point in setting a budget if you are going to spend whatever you want to spend. Budgets can be a pain to follow, but they are put in place to be an agent of change. Change in financial habits is a good thing—unless you are changing for the worse. In that case, you may need to reread letter 4 that details the beauty of discomfort.

My motto when working with a budget is, "Budget your budget!" Just because you set aside a certain amount to be spent doesn't mean you must spend it. If you can find savings or inexpensive alternatives, by all means, do so. A budget is meant as a guide to stop you from spending over a certain amount. It isn't a tool to give you the excuse to spend exactly that amount. The line should read up to $1,000, or no more than $1,000. It doesn't say, "Look, we have $1,000; let's blow it." Savings found within your budget can prove resourceful in the future when the unexpected occurs or when you have to double back due to a failed attempt. Money matters and nothing solidifies that more than a properly assembled budget. Having a budget when investing in your business could be the difference between a business that sees profits early on and a business that's unaware of its expenses and headed towards debt. There's no joy in not knowing where your money has gone. So in case you haven't figured it out already, my number-one financial business start-up recommendation is a budget.

What's in your wallet?

List your top 3 business expenses or top 3 expected expense. What's your plan?

_____

_____

_____

_____

_____

_____

_____

_____

_____

_____

_____

_____

_____

_____

_____

_____

_____

_____

_____

What good is an idea if it remains an idea? Try. Experiment. Iterate. Fail. Try again. Change the world.

— Simon Sinek, Author

3 Major Keys

Of someone were to walk up to you today and ask you about your business or dreams, would you be prepared with an elevator speech? An elevator speech is a thirty-second synopsis of your business or idea meant to draw the individual in, making them want to know more. If you aren't at that point, there are three key questions you should ask yourself. The first question you should ask is, "What is my business or idea?" Do you truly know what the business you want to build is? Do you have a full grasp of the idea you are ready to give birth to? There's nothing wrong with not having it all together when approaching an entrepreneurial endeavor; however, if you plan on advancing toward business, it's imperative you understand your business better than anyone else. When you speak of your business or idea, you should be able to speak with such conviction and belief that it causes those listening to want to know more. Many entrepreneurs have a general idea, but not many are sure exactly what it is they want to do or how the business will be structured. It's counterproductive to have a business logo, website, and marketing items without a clear understanding of your business and how it can impact the market. Case in point: I may not have a plethora of pictures on my social-media business pages; however, if you reach out to me or approach me about my businesses, I can speak with a level of conviction that has secured me every client thus far. I know what my businesses are, I know what services they yield, and I'm aware of how they can impact my target market.

The second question you must ask yourself is, "Who is my target market?" When my passion for events turned into a business, I was under the impression that every event would bring me the same joy and satisfaction. I quickly learned that that was not the case. An event as detailed and large as a wedding will not yield the same experience for me as an intimate gathering or children's party. Along the way, I had to find my niche and develop a way to market and profit from it. I'm a huge fan of elaborate children's parties and detailed intimate gatherings. There are ways to approach every celebration, and the path to those types of events brought me the most joy and satisfaction. When a potential client inquiries about those types of events, my pitch tends to have a more jubilant tone and presentation.

Now, I'm a major advocate of never leaving any coins on the table. That being said, I offer weddings and corporate-coordination packages as well. I give the same amount of time, creativity, and elegance to any event I oversee. Seeing the look on a bride's face after bringing her vision to life is a wedding planner's biggest reward. The process of planning those types of events brings me a different type of joy than others, but it continues to bring me joy. I learned that my target market is someone with a creative imagination who doesn't simply want an elegant event but wants a custom and unique experience. When marketing your business, it's important to be aware of who you are targeting.

The final question you must ask yourself is, "What is my purpose?" In finding your purpose, you find your motivation. Let's say you have chosen to start an event-planning business. Is your choice simply to plan events because you have determined you can order linens and balloons? Or have you decided to become an event planner because when someone mentions a Mickey Mouse–themed first-birthday party, your mind goes to layouts, colors, execution, and location? I know I'm operating within my purpose as event planner because the smiles and positive energy that I receive from every client I've designed experiences for sticks with me.

I rest easy after an event knowing that I've tailored an experience completely custom to my clients' wants, and they were pleased. Operating within my purpose is all the motivation I need to continue on the path of entrepreneurship.

Defining your business, acknowledging your target market, and fulfilling your purpose are three major keys to success. Ask yourself these questions, and write your responses over and over until it clicks. Most small businesses fail because of lack of knowledge that yields longevity. Success is great, but a successful entrepreneur should desire to have longevity in his or her business and efforts. When moving forward on your path of entrepreneurship, make sure you can proclaim that you "have the keys."

Got keys?
Write a 30 sec elevator speech and use it to practice. Who/what is your market?

_____

_____

_____

_____

_____

_____

_____

_____

_____

_____

_____

_____

_____

_____

_____

_____

_____

_____

_____

In business, you don't get what you deserve, you get what you negotiate.

— *Anonymous*

Ask for It

ou have not because you ask not. This saying holds true to every word. We live in a society of give and take. It's the haves versus the have-nots, and to get what you want, you have to request it. No one is going to walk up to you and offer you money or support, so stop expecting it. Entrepreneurship comprises many different factors. To be an entrepreneur doesn't mean you have to build your business on your own. Now, I'm not saying to get a partner or give parts of your business or credit or notoriety away. I'm just saying you need to ask. Don't be afraid to seek out sponsorships to pour into your business or idea.

People don't mind investing in something they believe in or something they believe is a good cause. A sponsorship could free up a lot of your financial ties and be the difference between a subpar presentation and a proper presentation. Learn how to network. There's nothing wrong with asking to shadow someone or building a positive business relationship. Greeting someone with a smile and a handshake can turn a stranger into an asset for your growth and development. Later down the line, that connection can take your business, idea, or design to the next level. Its human nature to complain about what you don't have or to complain about what someone isn't doing. Take an honest assessment of yourself. What have you done to entice people into action?

Learn to ask for what you want. Yes, I said "want." Simply asking for what you need may not yield the result you were expecting. Thus, my recommendation is to *always* ask for exactly what you want. Here is an example: Let's say you are preparing for a launch event, and you are soliciting sponsors. You reach out to a beverage company and ask them to sponsor your event by sending items to accommodate two hundred people. As a sponsor, they see this and decide to send you promotional or marketing items for two hundred people. It's a smaller version of their products or even coupons, and it helps them drive business.

You receive the items, and although grateful, you are disappointed and left without an essential element for your event. See, in your mind, when you reached out to the beverage company, you wanted them to send enough beverages to accommodate two hundred people at your event. This is an expense you could've eliminated. However, you were not clear in your request. Had you asked for what you wanted, the outcome may have been different.

You might have said, "Hello, I'm hosting a launch event for my business [insert business and event details] and expecting a guest count of two hundred. [Insert comment about the beverage company's position in the community and a compliment about their brand.] Your sponsorship of beverages to accommodate the guests at the event would be a wonderful addition and greatly appreciated."

This difference in request makes a difference in the response. In the abbreviated example, there are details and specific requests that should guide the potential sponsor's decision. Asking for what you want doesn't only pertain to sponsorships. Learning to ask for what you want is a general rule of thumb that can be applied in many situations.

What is it you want?
List one or two vendors or businesses that you could help you get to where you desire to be. How would you request assistance?

_____

_____

_____

_____

_____

_____

_____

_____

_____

_____

_____

_____

_____

_____

_____

_____

_____

_____

We are all faced with a series of great opportunities brilliantly disguised as impossible situations.

— *Charles R. Swindoll, Author*

Move Over

Get out of your own way. I'm sure you have heard this many times before, but I'm saying it again. Your biggest critic is often yourself. Standing in the way of your blessings and potential allows you to become a victim of defeat. Inside each of us is a gift. It's our responsibility to discover that gift and use it properly. When things aren't going the way we hoped, we shouldn't become our own demise. God didn't give us our gifts without providing an instruction manual. Sometimes it takes a problem for us to sit down, read the instructions, and proceed with clarity. If you have never assembled a bike before, you understand that you aren't going to be able to successfully assemble it on the first attempt without direction. The same can be said with business and idea building.

As an entrepreneur, you are new to your business or idea. You don't have all the answers, and no matter how far you go, you can always use direction. Step to the side, and seek the answers you need. Don't stand in the way of your growth and greatness because you are allowing failure and fear to take over. A great disappointment in my entrepreneurial journey came from a delay I caused by standing in my own way. I look at where I am today and where I am headed, and I smile. I also look at where I was and where I could be if I would have gotten out of my own way. We like to pacify our delays by saying, "It was not God's timing" or "Delayed but not denied." Although both statements could be true, there's also the regret of time wasted. When we delay our dreams, we aren't denying success, however, we are denying ourselves the potential to be so much more, right where we're standing.

There's no better time than right now, right where you are. I had to learn that the hard way. Stop blocking your advancement by telling yourself it could be better later. It could be better later, but it could also be better right now. Never rush toward anything; however, if the timing is right, and you are capable of succeeding, don't wait. Arm yourself with a faith so strong that you wake up every morning ready to accomplish every task you approach. You may fail at half of them, but your faith allowed you to move, which allowed you to learn. Lessons in entrepreneurship often lead to increase. The goal in dream chasing is increase, so learn to move on over.

Get out the way!
What are you holding yourself back from?

_____

_____

_____

_____

_____

_____

_____

_____

_____

_____

_____

_____

_____

_____

_____

_____

_____

_____

_____

_____

_____

_____

Early to bed, early to rise, work like hell and advertise.

— *Ted Turner, Entrepreneur and Businessman*

Blessings in Darkness

The biggest blessings and moments of enlightenment can come from darkness. Moments in the dark force you to focus and adjust so that you can see your way through. While going through the rough patches of building your business, although you may feel defeated, your vision is most clear. During this time, you are being strengthened, and things are working for your good. You have to change your way of thinking and allow yourself to find the good in the bad. There are some things that need darkness to flourish. Tap into your talents, and develop within you that which can only be achieved in the dark.

Vision realignment is a gift that comes from darkness. Getting comfortable in business or efforts is common, and we may need to be forced to turn things around. Dark places provide the platform to think outside the box and see things differently. Realignment comes from struggle and hardship when it seemed like there were fewer yeses and more nos. You can't reach your full potential from light alone. The light brings comfort and assurance, but the true blessing comes from discomfort. Discomfort for an entrepreneur is like a ram in the bush. You will either take this time to push your way through, or you will give up.

Entrepreneurs walking in their calling would not consider giving up, so learn to celebrate the dark.

When you step out of the darkness into the blessings provided for you, your outlook will be totally different. Things that used to bother or discourage you will not be a factor anymore. Surviving darkness will give you confidence that nothing can defeat you. Looking back over things, you will realize that you have been through way too much to let insignificant things throw you off your game. Stop complaining. If God can bless you in the dark, he's prepared to bless you where you are. Small things are nothing to a giant, and that's the mind frame you need to maintain to continue on your entrepreneurial journey. Be cheerful in everything so that negativity doesn't taint your endeavors. The dark is never a place we aspire to be. We want to do well and excel to great heights. There's no great climb without obstacles along the way. Instead of looking down or back to where you were, look up and celebrate the beauty waiting at the top. There are many blessings and lessons in the dark. I dare you to allow yourself to receive them.

Are you afraid of the dark?
How are you preparing yourself for the dark times in entrepreneurship?
Have you already experienced them? If so, how'd you manage?

_____

_____

_____

_____

_____

_____

_____

_____

_____

_____

_____

_____

_____

_____

_____

_____

_____

_____

If Plan A doesn't work, the alphabet has 25 more letters.

— Claire Cook, Author

Turn the Page

Such a simple notion met with harsh realities. You gathered the strength to make it through your dark times and receive your blessings; however, you can't help but reflect back to your time in the light. A time when things were good—or so you thought. A time when you could map out your future, and you knew everything was going to be all right. For most entrepreneurs, that time comes when they decide to step out on faith and chase their dreams. They envision how things will be and how much of a success they plan to become. Things may go well initially, but in the blink of an eye, a change comes around that knocks the wind out of their bodies. The setbacks become apparent, and the darkness sets in.

Take control of your destiny by realizing you aren't there anymore. You made it out of the dark, so why is it so hard to turn the page? The next chapter of any great book can't begin until the page has been turned. Despite any hardships you may go through, God has a plan for you that's bigger than any plan you have for yourself, but he can't bless you if you are stuck on the same page. On the same page, in the same spot, reflecting on what was instead of rejoicing over what is to come. You must let go of the bitterness and set aside the self-pity so that you can heal. Setbacks are not the end. Setbacks bring new beginnings and restoration.

In my darkest hour, I remained grateful. If you can't be grateful for what you have and where you are, you will not appreciate where God is trying to take you. See, I was simply grateful for the opportunity to do what I love. I suffered hardships, compared my talents and abilities to others, and began to doubt that I should even continue. There were times when I had so much vision but so little business. I continued to work and invest in my craft, keeping the faith that my time would come. Because I could keep my faith, God stepped in to do the work for me. I received clients I never anticipated. I also learned to utilize all my skills and generate revenue in different ways.

I turned the page! I shook off all the feelings of failure, doubt, and defeat. I'm taking my steps toward my finish line, prepared to face whatever comes my way. It's hard not to miss what you once had or forget the bad that caused you pain, but it's necessary. Everything that happens to you along your journey is necessary for you to grow. You may have been comfortable before, but God wants to take you higher. Turn the page, and step out of the dark. Walk in your purpose toward the peace you deserve.

So you're doing this?

By this point in the book, you should have a mind full of entrepreneurial thoughts. Are you ready to continue the journey and reap the rewards?

Secure

Moments Create Momentum

Growth is your friend, so secure that bag.

Budget, Base, & Blinders

y top 3 B's for business. Separately each of these is great, but the marriage of them all makes them that much better. Earlier in the book, I discussed my viewpoints on the importance of a budget. I won't spend too much time on my first B here. However, I'll dig a little deeper. We all have that one friend who invests time in planning and preparing, just to throw it all out the window when things switch up. Are you that friend? Do you know that friend? Budget preparation can be viewed the same way.

You have invested time, energy, and efforts in tailoring a budget for your goals. It's all too easy to toss that budget once you begin making profit or think you can handle things a different way. Remember, a budget is a moving document. If things switch up, switch up the budget. People tend to believe that a budget is only necessary when you're trying to piece those last 3 pennies together. No! The more you make, the more you should budget. You should be able to see where your money is going and how it's being managed. Business can change at any moment, and you don't want to be stuck in a situation that you can't handle because you chose not to budget your money.

A good budget is like the fries straight out of the grease at McDonald's. It looks good and makes us feel good. Another take on budgets I'd like to present is how other vendors approach them. If you are preparing to work with another vendor and they don't discuss a budget with you, take that as a mental note. It may prove to be difficult to work with someone that doesn't handle business similar to you. The easy resolution to keep the business transactions flowing is to mention a budget to them. Be upfront with them about where you stand and what your plan is. The vendor should receive it well, and it may even entice them to compile a budget and do the same.

It's all about that base. Base, foundation, early beginnings, or whatever you'd like to call it, is essential to growth. The base of your idea, concept, business, endeavors, etc. is what keeps you grounded as you reach the highs of your journey. Once an entrepreneur has begun to pick up steam, they are quick to review how they started and what they would like to change. At this stage in the journey, a rebranding is being contemplated. Rebranding is good for business if done properly. It lets the consumer know you are going places and you have fresh ideas and product offerings.

Outgrowing your start is typical. Embrace the change and make the moves that best benefit your business or brand. It's possible, however, to rebrand without throwing away your base. The core of what you believe and stand on is what makes your business. Keep your base strong and continue to build on it. You can renovate the house as much as you need to, but make sure you keep that base strong. As long as you have something to build on, you'll never run out of ideas. The most important thing is to stay focused.

Have you ever had a project you were trying to complete and every time you turned around there was something to distract you? Your entrepreneurial journey is the same way. Initially, you are so excited about starting your business, and you put your time and energy into trying to get things going. No one told you how much work it would be along the way and that the higher you get, the more focused you needed to be. Distractions will come in many forms, and before you know it, you will have lost days, months, and years on your journey. Put your blinders on and block out all the things that will keep you from being great. If it isn't contributing to your plan, you need to block it out. With a steady budget, solid base, and sturdy blinders, you set your ceiling and control your pace.

Can you vibe?
List ways you can implement the 3 B's in your business plan. What do you need to focus on?

_____

_____

_____

_____

_____

_____

_____

_____

_____

_____

_____

_____

_____

_____

_____

_____

_____

It's often best to just mind your own business.

-LaKeshia Marie

Lane Management

You can't see where you are going if you are always focused on someone or something else. Learn how to mind your business. And when I say "your business," I don't just mean avoid "being nosy"; I mean the business you have devoted time to building. Stay in your own lane, which consists of where you started, where you are, and where you would like to be. Managing your own lane will ultimately place you in a position to excel without the unnecessary drama, stress, and distractions that come with peeking into someone else's lane.

I know it's hard not to wonder why this person is doing better than you or why they have things that you don't, but that isn't your burden to bear. Have you ever considered that maybe they are where they are because they learned early on to manage their lane? It has been said before, and I'm a firm believer, that you can't compete where you don't compare. Your competition isn't in the lane beside you. Your competition is right there in your lane with you—standing in the thick of it, challenging you to do more, work harder, and think larger. Peeking into someone else's lane can take you off a course that was designed specifically for you. God has a plan for each of us, and I guarantee he didn't leave your blessing in your neighbor's lane.

We live in a social-media-driven society. The facades of lavish lifestyles and success cause us to have blurred vision and make irresponsible decisions. You must learn to decipher between fallacy and reality. Separate yourself from the noise. It's possible to draw inspiration or enjoyment from someone else, but all that can be done while remaining in your lane. What I mean by that is to support someone else or even be inspired by them. You don't have to leave your space and travel into theirs. I believe it's important to stay centered in your lane and soak in the good around you. Once you wander out of your lane into someone else's, you are giving attention to their progress, whether good or bad, and your lane has been left unattended. Now, when you return to your lane, you bring back things that have no business being there.

As an entrepreneur, your primary focus should be what you are building. Work with others, learn from others, and grow with others, all while remembering to stay in your lane. It isn't an easy concept to grasp because it's hard not to get drawn in. I can speak from experience that when I began to venture out of my lane, I became confused as to my direction. I was not sure of where I wanted to go or what I wanted to be. I spent too much time in lanes that were not mine, and I decided I wanted my lane to look like theirs. I opened the door for comparison, which delayed my growth and exposure because I didn't understand the importance of lane management. To win a race and keep the pace, a runner should never turn his or her head to look behind or side to side. If the runner is going to win, he or she must win in the assigned lane. It doesn't matter what is going on in the other lanes. All that matters is that the runner gives it all in the given lane.

Are you minding yours?
List ways you believe you can keep comparison and other peoples' success and/or failures from impacting your entrepreneurial progress.

_____

_____

_____

_____

_____

_____

_____

_____

_____

_____

_____

_____

_____

_____

_____

_____

_____

_____

Act enthusiastic, and you will be enthusiastic.

— *Dale Carnegie, Author, and Motivational Speaker*

The Optics

S ometimes it isn't about how you presented it; it's about how they received it. How did it look? I'll never forget hearing the word "optics" being used in plain speech. I was watching a movie, and the actress proceeded to validate her color choices because they would be best for "the optics." I chuckled to myself because she could've simply said "pictures," but she chose to finesse the situation and say "optics." "Optics" is a classy word. Its original intent was to describe the scientific method in which sight reacts to the behavior of light. It has since been used to reference the way in which an event or action is received by those in public.

It's important that the optics remain in your favor. It is okay to make mistakes, and things will go wrong; however, those things that you can control should be controlled. The public translates to income for an entrepreneur, so how your business is perceived can determine your success, failure, and stability. Remember that from this point on, you are building a brand. Along with a brand comes a reputation. Some of the things you used to do you simply will not be able to do anymore. You will have to carry yourself as an example of how you would like your business to resonate. You would not go clock into your nine-to-five and cut up, so while you are on your twenty-four-hour clock, be mindful of "the optics."

This doesn't mean drastically changing who you are or being "fake," as they say. Simply put, it's making wise business decisions and better choices so that you can grow from where you once were. Change isn't a bad thing. This is something that shouldn't have to be explained in 2018. If a person isn't changing, then he or she isn't growing. Personally, I don't want to be around a bunch of stuck individuals. It doesn't matter how "real," they think they are; if they aren't willing to change, they are just stuck. Being an entrepreneur who knows the struggle of change and transition, I can't see myself giving my hard-earned money to a "stuck" or stagnate business, with an owner just the same.

Stop saying you don't care what other people think about you! Yes, you do—at least, you should. Entrepreneurship doesn't afford you the luxury of disregarding "the optics" and not caring about what other people see or think. Foolish money doesn't make money, and not being aware of how your actions strike others is foolish. There's a difference between a premature opinion and constructive criticism. Not everyone who has something to say about you or your business is a hater. The consumer is simply stating why he or she would not want to continue business with you and what may need to be changed. You don't have to fall in line with every suggestion or criticism you receive, but acknowledge the perception and move forward. There's no perfect business, but there are businesses that sell themselves short because they choose to disregard their behavior.

How are you moving?

Are you moving in a way that highlights your business and potential?

What methods and/or actions could you implement?

_____

_____

_____

_____

_____

_____

_____

_____

_____

_____

_____

_____

_____

_____

_____

_____

_____

_____

Logic will get you from A to B. Imagination will take you everywhere.

—Albert Einstein, Physicist

Committed

Finding your passion is nice, and walking in your purpose is even better. The time will come after the hard work is underway that you must ask yourself just how committed you are to continuing your journey. The peace comes from realizing you are doing what you love, and you are blessed enough to do it well. When the work gets tough, you determine just how committed you are. Entrepreneurial endeavors require 110 percent commitment. You can't do well in your business by being inconsistent in your drive and commitment. If you aren't ready to give your all to your journey, it may be time to reconsider the journey.

Entrepreneurship isn't the ideal situation to start and stop at your leisure. The hard work, research, and time invested are worth it once you can taste success. Commitment isn't a choice for an entrepreneur. Commitment is a must. Being committed, along with hard work and discipline, directs you toward a win—an appreciation for success as you continue your journey. The quality of your business or the product you represent is in direct proportion to how committed you have been, are, and will be. When you are passionate and committed to your purpose, anything is possible.

The only limits you have are the ones you place on yourself. Stay committed to your vision and goals. Pair your commitment with an honest effort, and there's no reason your goals can't come to fruition. To achieve something you have never had, you must commit time to doing things you have never done. When your efforts seem to be in vain, or you are tired of where you are on your journey, research other methods, and explore your options. It isn't easy to commit yourself fully to things in life, but it's possible. Those who are sincere about being an entrepreneur will do what needs to be done to be successful. Get committed, and stay committed. You owe it to yourself.

Stay.

What will you do to ensure you stay true to your dreams and goals?

_____

_____

_____

_____

_____

_____

_____

_____

_____

_____

_____

_____

_____

_____

_____

_____

_____

_____

_____

_____

Screw it, let's do it.

— *Richard Branson, Founder of Virgin Group*

Up Next

Whew! We have made it to the conclusion. The journey from passion to peace toward your dreams isn't an easy one, but it doesn't have to be complicated either. There's never an end in entrepreneurship. What you create and what you own can last forever. It's time to evaluate where you are and what you have done. What type of entrepreneur do you want to be? Work toward building something so great that one day it works for you. Transition that active income to passive income, and chase a new dream. Make yourself a list, and determine what is up next. You may want to expand your business or start another business to tap into your other talents. Whatever it's you decide to do, be sure that you don't allow yourself to become stagnant. Entrepreneurship is a beautiful complexity, and the opportunities are limitless. I encourage you all to have a plan and to always consider what could happen next.

There's no timetable for entrepreneurial success. It isn't a race; it's simply a journey. Setting goals and looking for the next step is encouragement to stay on your course and in your lane. Goals and dreams make getting up each day a bit more refreshing. Just because you may have made it or are well on your way doesn't mean there aren't a few more steps for you to take. Look at yourself in the mirror, and affirm that you are up next. Your time is the most valuable resource you have. Don't waste it by sleeping on all that greatness. Take painful risks, look fear in the face, and go be amazing!

Be great.

What did this book do for you? What, as a whole, can you take away from this read?

_____

_____

_____

_____

_____

_____

_____

_____

_____

_____

_____

_____

_____

_____

_____

_____

_____

_____

A Final Letter to You

Entrepreneurship is more than a fad. Today, I see more and more people deciding to step outside their comfort zones and invest in themselves. There's such a reward in having your own and building your own. Passion is the fire inside each of us that ignites the will to want to step outside our box. I believe that passion can take you much further than imagination. Passion drives and grants you the opportunity for discovery. While exploring your passions, be open to what is revealed.

Purpose gives us definition. Finding your purpose in life makes life that much sweeter. A life with purpose is a life well lived. I'm grateful for my purpose, and you should be grateful too. After being in corporate America for a while after graduation, I knew I was meant to be and do so much more. Don't be afraid to accept your purpose, and don't get confused as to what your purpose truly is. Chase those dreams, and utilize your talents. You deserve the win, and we deserve to be blessed with all that it's you have to offer. God doesn't make mistakes, and he has blessed each of us with a unique purpose and a task to do our part.

Entrepreneurship isn't for everyone, but for those who fit into this category, there's such a peace about doing what you love. Being able to do what you love and get paid for it almost seems too good to be true. We become complacent in the corporate sector, building someone else's dreams while dreading the Monday-morning clock-in. You can have peace that pays your bills, and walking in your calling can provide that. Peace comes just in time during your journey and transcends the rest of the way.

My hope is that you find what you need in the words written in each letter. You don't have to be *the* expert to share with others; you just have to have lived and experienced enough to pass insight along. This is my experience along the way. I wanted to encourage others who may feel like me or be more successful than me to simply keep going. I believe in you, and I hope you have learned to believe in you too. I look forward to being your customer.

Sincerely,

LaKeshia Marie

Acknowledgments

First and foremost, I would like to give honor to God. He has blessed me in so many ways and is the driving force behind everything I attempt to do. To my parents, Claudette and Jerome Barbee, I'm thankful for the life you have given me and the respect you have for my life choices and goals. Not only do you support me with words, but you also support me as customers—never asking for a discount, even when I try to give one, and always being available when I need you. I'm grateful for your love.

Briona Laneé, you are my heart. I know I don't have to tell you that, but you deserve to hear it. You are more than a younger sister to me; you are a friend and a young woman I admire and am so very proud of. You are wise beyond your years, and I thank you for every conversation and critique. I know that it will not be long before you place your entrepreneurial stamp on things.

Byron, thank you for your patience and understanding. For pushing me when I pushed back and not allowing me to give up on my dreams. The time and patience you've invested in me means more to me than words could describe. You never once tried to stunt my growth or stop my shine. You let me chase my dreams as we built our life together, and for that I appreciate and love you.

Ebonie Ingram, our friendship is a journey, and I'm glad we've agreed to stay on the ride. You were the first person to lay eyes on my book in its rawest state. I appreciate the time and truth you consistently give me. Thank you for allowing me to be me and supporting my moves.

I'm grateful to have you as my porch-swing friend. Let's launch your business, I can't wait to see how far you go!

Natasha Montgomery Kendle, there aren't enough words to express the appreciation, admiration, and respect I have for you. You took me under your wing and helped me develop my craft, showing me that there was enough work out here for us all. You are an angel on earth. I admire your dedication, hard work, and commitment to me. You let me into your family and heart. For every time you have checked on me, fussed at me, and assisted me, I thank you.

To my J-Briggy, Jessica Brigance, you've been on this ride with me since middle school and you've never once tried to hop off. Since college, we've lived in different time zones but you've always made it a point to encourage and support me. You are my sister for life and I'm blessed to have someone as genuine and honest as you in my corner.

Last but not least, I thank Shavonne Greenwell and Cushena Scott. Cushena, you aren't only a boss; you are also a bleeding heart. Not once have you given me anything other than positive energy and light. You stepped into my life at the essential part of my journey, and I thank you for your friendship. I thank you for being so willing to assist me in my business development and for using your business platform to elevate or assist mine. I pray that you are blessed many times over for all that you do for others. You are the definition of a committed entrepreneur, and I applaud your shining example.

Shavonne, there would be no Panache by Marie Events without you. You support me in everything I do and with everything I do. You are the epitome of a best friend. I could write a book on our friendship alone, but you know what your friendship means to me. You can never leave, LOL. We have many more goals to reach, but we are on our way!

Made in the USA
Lexington, KY
17 August 2018